The Secrets

Magic

Tim Collins

WOW! facts

Badger Publishing Limited
Oldmedow Road,
Hardwick Industrial Estate,
King's Lynn PE30 4JJ
Telephone: 01438 791037

www.badgerlearning.co.uk

2 4 6 8 10 9 7 5 3 1

The Secrets of Magic ISBN 978-1-78464-018-7

Publisher: Susan Ross
Senior Editor: Danny Pearson
Publishing Assistant: Claire Morgan
Designer: Fiona Grant
Series Consultant: Dee Reid

Photos: Cover Image: © RubberBall/Alamy
Page 5: © Trigger Image/Alamy
Page 7: © Hale-Sutton Europe/Alamy
Page 8: Laura Cavanaugh/Getty Images
Page 9: APIC/Getty Images
Page 10: Courtesy Everett Collection/REX
Page 11: Buyenlarge/Buyenlarge/The LIFE Images Collection/Getty
Page 12: Archive Photos/Getty Images
Page 13: ITV/REX
Page 15: bennosix.com
Page 19: © Dario Lo Presti/Alamy
Page 20: Quinn Rooney/Getty Images
Page 21: © fStop/Alamy
Page 22: Ailli Schneider/REX
Page 23: Glenn Copus/REX
Page 24: REX
Page 25: Monty Brinton/CBS via Getty Images
Page 26: Picture Perfect/REX
Page 28: Ewing GallowayUIG/REX
Page 29: Paul Lovelace/REX
Page 30: © Jason/Alamy

Attempts to contact all copyright holders have been made.
If any omitted would care to contact Badger Learning, we will be happy to make appropriate arrangements.

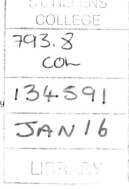

Contents

Vocabulary

audience	illusions
ditching	magicians
entertainment	miraculous
glamorous	switching

1. The history of magic

Magic was not always fun.

Long ago, doctors in Egypt tried to use magic to cure sick people.

In the Middle Ages, magicians were thought to be in touch with the devil.

Over time, magic stopped being something scary and became a form of entertainment.

People would go to street fairs to watch magicians perform simple tricks.

These magicians did tricks like pulling a coin out of an empty bag.

In the 19th Century magic changed again. Jean Robert-Houdin ordered two books on watch-making but the wrong books were sent. In the parcel were two books on magic.

Jean was amazed at the tricks described in the books and he began practising them.

After a few years he was so good at magic that he opened his own theatre for people to come and see his magic tricks.

For some of the 20th Century magic went out of fashion. People stopped going to theatres to watch magic shows.

Then magicians started doing magic on TV shows and millions of people could watch their amazing tricks. It became fashionable again.

Now street magic is popular again and thousands of people crowd into public places to see amazing magic tricks or illusions.

2. The great magicians

Chung Ling Soo

One magician called himself Chung Ling Soo.

He was killed on stage when a 'bullet trick' went wrong.
A fake gun fired for real and shot him.

Harry Houdini

He was famous for his miraculous escapes.

He would break free from strong chains in front of amazed crowds. One of his most daring tricks was to escape from handcuffs inside a large tank of water.

The slogan on one of his posters said: 'Failure means a drowning death.'

David Copperfield

The most successful magician in history is David Copperfield.

He has made over $4 billion performing his magic tricks.

People go to David Copperfield shows to watch his amazing illusions.

In 1983, in front of a crowd, he made the Statue of Liberty disappear! How did he do that?

Penn and Teller

Penn and Teller are famous for their gory magic acts.

In one act Teller appears to be run over by an 18-wheel truck!

They sometimes use fake blood to make it look like their tricks have gone wrong.

Cyril Takayama

Cyril Takayama does a special magic trick that really shocks his audience – he takes his head off!

It falls off his shoulders and the audience all gasp! How does he do that?

3. Magic skills

How do magicians do magic tricks?

Magicians are very clever at moving things so quickly that no one sees.

WOW! facts

Benno Six can just shake his leg and his shoelaces tie themselves in a neat bow!

Here are some of their skills:

Palming

If a magician needs to secretly hide something in his hand, he moves it from his fingers to the palm of his hand so quickly that the audience do not see him doing it.

This is known as palming.

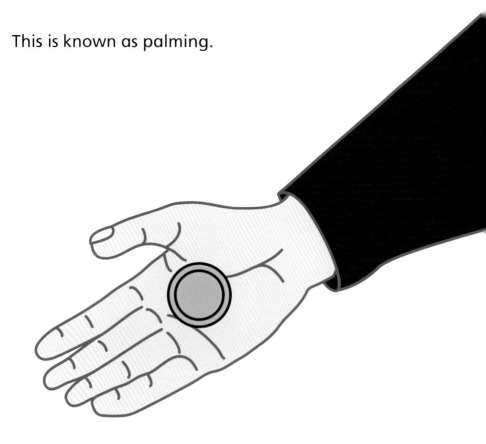

Switching

If a magician needs to swap one object for another, he does the swap so quickly that the audience do not see him doing it.

This is known as switching.

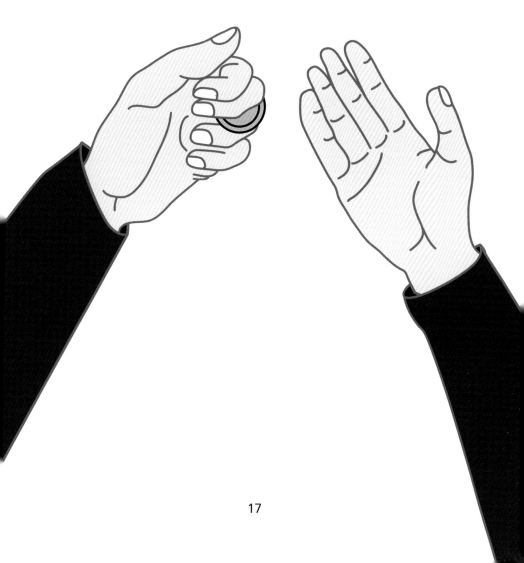

Ditching

Perhaps the magician needs to get rid of an object. He moves his hand so quickly that the audience do not see him doing it.

This is known as ditching.

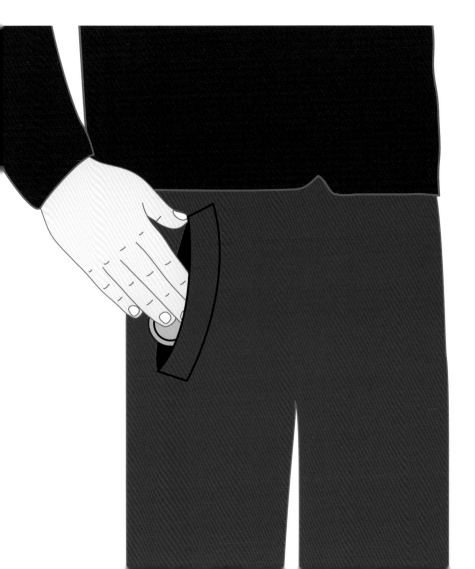

Good magicians practise these skills thousands and thousands of times until they can do them so quickly the audience doesn't see what is happening.

But just moving things quickly is not enough. Magicians have another trick.

They distract the audience so they are looking at something else while the palming or switching or ditching is done.

How do magicians distract their audience?

One way magicians distract the audience is by making a big movement with one hand so the audience do not notice the small movements they are making with the other hand.

But there are lots of other ways magicians distract their audience so they do not see what is really going on:

- Some wear dazzling suits.
- Some have glamorous assistants.
- Some do a lot of talking.

Siegfried and Roy were famous for performing with white tigers. Their show in Las Vegas was shut down when one of the tigers attacked Roy when he was on stage.

A magician called Criss Angel performed these illusions:

- swallowing razorblades
- bringing dead bodies back to life
- ripping people in half

Some pop stars have used magic illusions on stage. Michael Jackson invented a type of shoe that slotted into the floor and let him lean forward at an extreme angle.

4. Street magic

Magicians are always looking for new tricks to wow their audiences.

David Blaine had some new ideas for magic tricks. He spent 44 days inside a glass box! Everyone could see him and could see that he had no food.

How did he do that?

A magician called Dynamo performed an amazing trick.

It looked as though he was just rising up off the ground.

Another time it looked as though he was walking across the River Thames. How did he do that?

5. The secrets of magic

WARNING: If you think magic tricks should remain secret, DO NOT read these pages.

Trick: A woman in a long gown lies down in front of a curtain and the magician seems to make her float in the air.

How it's done: The long gown hides a secret platform attached to a mechanism behind the curtain that lifts her up.

Trick: A street magician asks someone to pick a card and show it to everyone except him.

Then the magician throws the pack of cards at a window and the chosen card sticks to the other side of the glass.

How it's done: An assistant waits on the other side of the glass with an identical pack of cards. They see the card as the volunteer shows it round, and stick it to their side of the window.

Trick: The magician's assistant lies inside a cabinet and is cut in half by a giant saw.

How it's done: The assistant is curled up in the top half and the legs sticking out the bottom half are fake. Or the assistant's body is actually inside a secret compartment in the table beneath the cabinet.

Trick: The magician gathers a rope into a loop and cuts it in half. He twists the ends together and the rope is complete again.

How it's done: The magician has a separate loop of rope hidden in his palm. This was the piece he cut.

Trick: A bullet is fired through a pane of glass at the magician, who catches it in his teeth.

How it's done: The magician is using a fake gun that only looks like it's being fired. The glass is shattered by a small explosion.

The magician hides the bullet in his hand while pretending to load the gun and then he slips the bullet into his mouth.

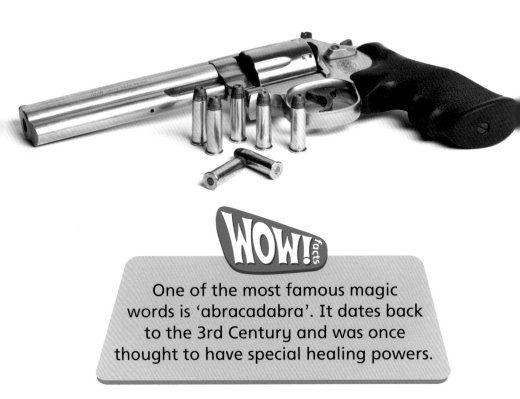

WOW! facts

One of the most famous magic words is 'abracadabra'. It dates back to the 3rd Century and was once thought to have special healing powers.

Questions

What was the subject of the books that Jean Robert-Houdin ordered? *(page 7)*

Which magic trick killed Chung Ling Soo? *(page 9)*

Who is the most successful magician in history and how much money has he made? *(page 12)*

Name two ways a magician distracts his audience. *(page 21)*

What river did Dynamo walk on? *(page 25)*

What does a magician hide in his hand while performing the bullet trick? *(page 30)*

Index